NATIONA
GEOGRAI

Looking for a New House

Nick Bruce

Our family is too big for our house.

Mom and dad say that we need to move.

We look for a new home.

We look at a house.

It has two bedrooms.

I like this house.

Dad says we need a bigger house.

We need a house that has three bedrooms.

We look at another house.

 It has three bedrooms.

I like this house.

4

Mom says we need a house
that is closer to her work.

We look at another house.

✓ It has three bedrooms.

✓ It is close to mom's work.

I like this house.

Dad says the house is too old.

It will need too much work.

We look at another house.

 It has three bedrooms.

 It is close to mom's work.

 It is not too old.

I like this house.

Mom says we need a house
that has a place to park her car.

We look at another house.

- ☑ It has three bedrooms.
- ☑ It is close to mom's work.
- ☑ It is not too old.
- ☑ It has a place to park mom's car.

I like this house.

My sister says we need a house
that has a yard to play in.

We look at another house.

 It has three bedrooms.

 It is close to mom's work.

 It is not too old.

 It has a place to park mom's car.

 It has a yard to play in.

I like this house.

Dad says this house is very new.

It costs too much.

We look at another house.

- ✔ It has three bedrooms.
- ✔ It is close to mom's work.
- ✔ It is not too old.
- ✔ It has a place to park mom's car.
- ✔ It has a yard to play in.
- ✔ It doesn't cost too much.

I like this house.

We all like this house.

This will be our new home.